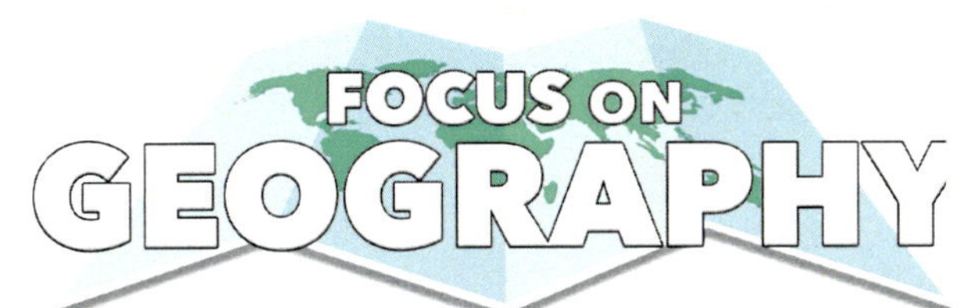

Focus on Japan

Ellen Rodger and Anne-Marie Rodger

A Crabtree Forest Book

Crabtree Publishing
crabtreebooks.com

Authors: Ellen Rodger and Anne Marie Rodger

Series research and development: Janine Deschenes

Editorial director: Kathy Middleton

Editor: Janine Deschenes

Proofreader: Melissa Boyce

Design: Tammy McGarr

IMAGE CREDITS

Shutterstock: Joshua Davenport front cover (top left); Benny Marty p 4 (top); KenSoftTH p 6 (top); kuremo p 6 (bottom); Distinctive Shots p 11 (bottom); beeboys p 13 (top right); Manuel Ascanio p 13 (bottom right); Muralonga p 14 (bottom left); Fly_and_Dive p 15 (top); image_vulture p 16 (top left); Photoerngo p 17 (bottom right); Kathy Matsunami p 17 (top); beibaoke p 20 (left); GC photographer p 21 (bottom); JoyCaym p 22 (left); Vladimir Zhoga p 23 (top); Bandit Chanheng p 27 (top); KPG-Payless p 28 (bottom); Ned Snowman p 28 (top), p 29 (middle); tackune p 29 (top); Ovu0ng p 29 (bottom); PixHound p 32 (top); marcociannarel p 32 (bottom); TokyoVideoStock p 35 (top); Osaze Cuomo p 35 (bottom); julianne p 36 (middle); Milosz Maslanka p 39 (middle right); akiyoko p 39 (middle left); Savvapanf Photo p 40 (top); Sean Pavone p 41 (top); Morumotto p 41 (bottom right); Media Whale Stock p 43 (top); cowardlion p 43 (middle); marcobrivio.photography p 43 (bottom)

Creative Commons: Tomohide shimura p 9 (top); p 19 (top left); 663highland p 19 (bottom); Wellcome Images p 23 (bottom right); p 28 (middle)

Wikimedia Commons: United States Public Domain, Shunsai Toshimasa p 18 (top); United States Public Domain Ginko Adachi p 20 (right); Public Domain Tokyo National Museum p 23 (middle); United States Public Domain Antares Historia p 24 (top);Public Domain_Imperial Household Agency p 25 (bottom); Department of Defense_Public Domain p 25 (top); Public Domain_U.S. Army_Lt. Gaetano Faillace p 26 (top left)

All other images from Shutterstock

Crabtree Publishing

crabtreebooks.com **800-387-7650**

In Canada: We acknowledge the financial support of the Government of Canada through the Canada Book Fund for our publishing activities.

Hardcover 978-1-0398-4293-9
Paperback 978-1-0398-4301-1
Ebook (pdf) 978-1-0398-4308-0
Epub 978-1-0398-4314-1

Published in Canada
Crabtree Publishing
616 Welland Avenue
St. Catharines, Ontario
L2M 5V6

Published in the United States
Crabtree Publishing
347 Fifth Avenue
Suite 1402-145
New York, New York, 10016

Library and Archives Canada Cataloguing in Publication
Available at Library and Archives Canada

Library of Congress Cataloging-in-Publication Data
Available at the Library of Congress

Printed in the USA/062024/CG20240201

Contents

Introduction

A Snapshot of a Busy City

What is it like living in the most **populous** city in the world? It's busy. Really busy. With more than 38 million people, the Greater Tokyo Area is considered a **metropolis**. It would take an entire day to walk it end to end. There are business districts with steel and glass high-rise buildings, neighborhoods with apartment blocks and schools, and markets teeming with shoppers. Luckily, nobody really needs to walk long distances in Tokyo. The city is known for its **efficient** public transit. Bus, subway, and train stops are all easily **accessible**.

Shibuya Station is one of the busiest railway stations in the world, with trains arriving every five minutes.

Shibuya Crossing, near Toyko's Shibuya railway station, is the busiest crosswalk in the world. It's so busy that it is described as a "scramble." As many as 3,000 people cross it every two minutes.

The city of Osaka is the 10th largest urban area in the world. Roughly 19 million people live in this financial center.

Down to Business

Japan, and Tokyo in particular, is a world center for business. The headquarters of some of the biggest companies on Earth are located there. Workers **commute** daily from other areas of the metropolis to work in the 23 wards and eight major business districts of Tokyo. More than 10 million people take the Tokyo Metro and Toei Subway each day. Some spend up to an hour and a half traveling back and forth from their homes to work.

Urban and Rural

Tokyo isn't Japan's only sprawling and heavily populated city. Yokohama, Osaka, and Nagoya clock in at around 2.2 to 3.7 million each. Most of Japan's big cities are located on the island of Honshu. It is the largest and most crowded of Japan's four main islands. About 92 percent of the population lives in cities. Rural Japan is much quieter and more traditional. It is also rapidly **depopulating**. Some smaller villages are disappearing. Most young people have left to live and work in the cities.

Agriculture is a big part of life in rural Japan, though available land is in short supply. Rice **paddies**, shown here, are a common sight.

Connected to Nature

One thing common throughout Japan's megacities and quieter villages is a historic connection to nature. Even in bustling city districts with busy shopping centers, bright with neon lights and noisy *pachinko* gaming parlors, a calming garden or **shrine** is just around the corner. These quiet spots are a link to the past and to the Japanese love of landscape, trees, and animals.

Wabi-sabi

Japan has undergone rapid transformation over the last 80 years. It is a thoroughly modern country with a long history and deep connection to the past. One ancient idea that has been maintained and modified in busy, modern Japan is *wabi-sabi*. Wabi-sabi influences many parts of everyday life. It is a world view that sees wisdom in nature and simplicity. Wabi-sabi is reflected in Japanese gardens, art, pottery, poetry, and traditional architecture. It emphasizes an appreciation for the forces of nature. This means that things such as bare winter tree branches or cracks in a piece of pottery are viewed as flawed but natural beauty.

Even fast-paced, modern cities maintain a link to the past and traditional culture with shrines and temples, green spaces, and historic areas.

Japanese gardens are often designed using the principles of wabi-sabi, including the idea that nothing is perfect.

Japan is a series of islands in East Asia, between the Pacific Ocean and the East Sea, or Sea of Japan.

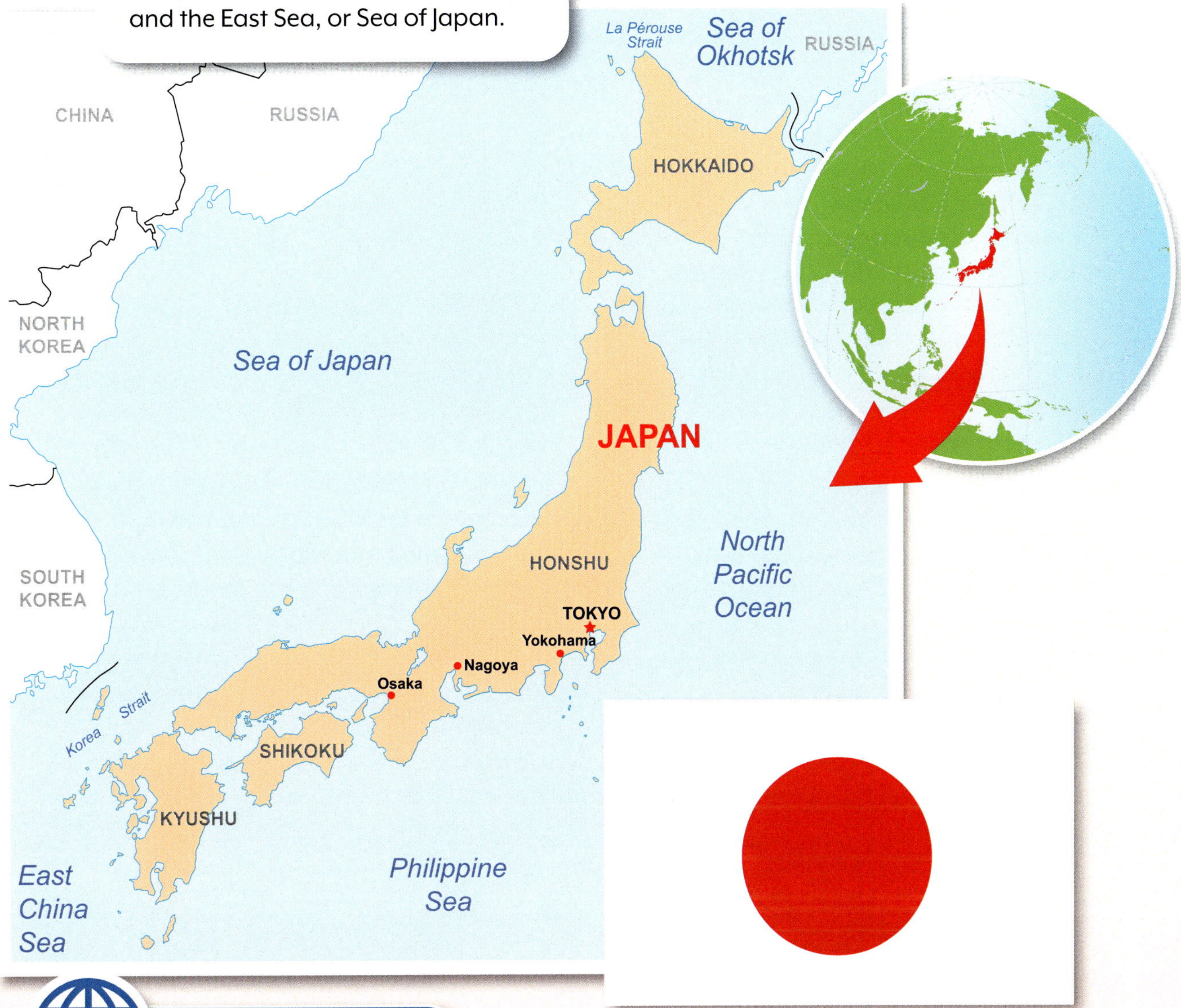

- **OFFICIAL NAME:** Japan, or, in Japanese, Nippon or Nihon
- **NATIONAL CAPITAL:** Tokyo
- **POPULATION:** 124,285,000
- **OFFICIAL LANGUAGE:** Japanese
- **LAND AREA:** 145,936 square miles (377,974 sq. km)

Surrounded by Sea

Japan has many neighbors and is connected to several different bodies of water. North and South Korea and southeastern Siberia, an area of Russia, are across the Sea of Japan. The La Pérouse Strait separates the northern islands of Japan from Russia. The East China Sea lies between Japan and China to the southwest. The east and south of Japan are bordered by the Pacific Ocean and the Philippine Sea.

CHAPTER 1

The Land

Japan is an archipelago, or group of islands, spread out in the Pacific Ocean from the Sea of Okhotsk in the northeast to the Philippine Sea in the southwest. The archipelago is made up of 14,125 islands. These islands—some small and some large— stretch over 1,900 miles (3,057 km). This makes Japan the largest island country in East Asia, with the sixth longest coastline in the world.

Most of Japan's islands are **uninhabited**. It's estimated that around 400 have people living on them.

Mainland Japan

The Japanese archipelago includes four larger islands that form what is called mainland Japan. This is where most of Japan's population lives and where most of its **industry** is located. From largest to smallest, these islands are: Honshu, Hokkaido, Kyushu, and Shikoku. Honshu is the most populous island, with 104 million residents. It is also where Tokyo, the country's capital city, is located. Hokkaido is the second-largest mainland island. It is separated from Honshu by the Tsugaru Strait. Kyushu is the third largest and farthest south of the mainland islands. It is an island of mountains and home to Japan's most active volcano, Mount Aso. Shikoku, the smallest of the main islands, is 140 miles (225 km) long and is home to almost 4 million people.

Osaka, on Honshu, is a large port city and **commercial** center. A port is a place where ships are loaded and unloaded.

The Bonin Islands are so isolated that wildlife has evolved differently from island to island. Many **native** plant species are found there. The Bonin white-eye bird (above) is a threatened species.

Hashima, or Gunkanjima, is an abandoned coal mining island off the coast of Nagasaki. Its undersea coal mines stopped production and workers who lived there left in 1974. It is now a **UNESCO World Heritage Site**.

Outer Islands

Japan has so many islands that in 2023, the country's Geospatial Information Authority re-counted them using photographs taken from the air and digital maps. The new tally of 14,125 islands is 7,273 more than the last survey done in 1987. The smallest islands have no human residents. Some islands have humid, **subtropical** climates. Others have warm summers and cold winters. Some are located far away from mainland Japan.

The Bonin or Ogasawara Islands, for example, are 26 hours from Tokyo by ship. They are a group of 30 small islands known for their forests, plants, and diversity of wildlife and birds. Only about 2,500 people live there today.

The Kuril Islands, near Hokkaido, were taken over by the **Soviet Union** after **World War II** (WWII). Japan still claims the four most southern Kuril Islands, which it calls its Northern Territories. Many **Indigenous** Ainu and Nivkh people live there.

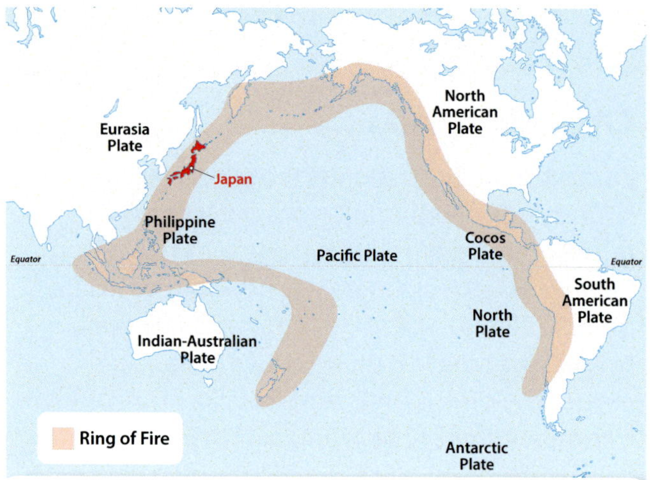

Most of Earth's volcanoes are located along the 24,855-mile (40,000 km) Ring of Fire. Ten percent of the world's active volcanoes are in Japan.

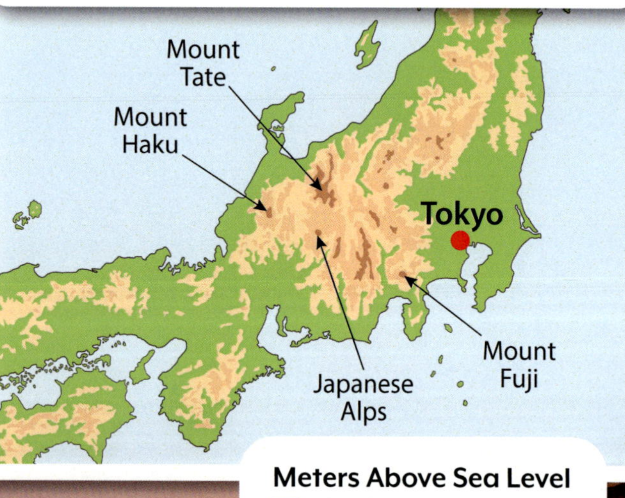

Japan's Terrain

Mountains and volcanoes—some of them active—dominate much of Japan's terrain. The country sits on the western edge of the Ring of Fire. This is a horseshoe-shaped area on the Pacific Ocean's rim where Earth's constantly-shifting **tectonic plates** often slide beneath each other. This sliding causes volcanic activity and many earthquakes. Japan is one of the most volcanically active places on Earth, with 111 volcanoes.

Most of Japan's mountains formed as volcanoes. Mount Fuji, Japan's most famous and highest volcano, rises to an impressive 12,388 feet (3,776 m). Known as *Fuji-san*, it has become a symbol of Japan. It is also a UNESCO World Heritage site. Mount Fuji, Mount Haku, also a UNESCO World Heritage Site, and Mount Tate make up the Three Holy Mountains of Japan. All are located on Honshu. The three mountains are considered traditionally **sacred** places to the people of Japan.

Mount Fuji towers behind Tokyo, 62 miles (100 km) southwest of the city. Many people climb the volcano—some for recreation and some as a spiritual act.

Japanese macaques, or snow monkeys, live in forests on Honshu, Shikoku, and Kyushu. Some are famous for their fondness of bathing in mountain hot springs. There are more than 27,000 **geothermal** hot springs in Japan.

Crops grow near the banks of the Mogami, a fast-flowing river on Honshu.

The Shinano River has five power dams and is also used for irrigation.

Japanese Alps

The mountainous terrain of Japan includes the Japanese Alps. Also known as "the roof of Japan," they are a series of mountain ranges that run through the mainland island of Honshu. There are three main groups in the Japanese Alps: the Hida Mountains, or Northern Alps, the Kiso Mountains, or Central Alps, and the Akaishi Mountains, or Southern Alps. These mountains reach an elevation of up to 9,842 feet (3,000 m).

Mountain Rivers

Japan's mountains fall into valleys where melting snow creates runoff that merges with rivers throughout Japan. Many of Japan's rivers are short and flow down steep **gradients** into flat **plains** and agricultural areas. These rivers, and the lakes some flow into, provide water for cities and towns, industrial use, and agricultural **irrigation**. At 228 miles (367 km) long, the Shinano River is Japan's largest and widest river. Located on Honshu, it flows from the foothills of Mount Kobushi in the Japanese Alps and joins several other rivers. The Shinano is the water source for Japan's first hydroelectric power plant, built in the 1920s.

Inland Lakes

Japan has about 100 lakes of various sizes. Some are less than 0.38 square miles (1 sq. km) in size. Lake Biwa, on Honshu, is the largest at 259 square miles (670 sq. km). It is also the oldest. Scientists date it back 5 million years. The "Fuji Five" are lakes that surround Mount Fuji: Lakes Kawaguchiko, Saiko or Sai, Yamanakako, Sojiko, and Motosuko. They were formed from the mountain's ancient lava eruptions that blocked rivers. They sit about 3,220 feet (980 m) above sea level. Some are surrounded by forests, such as Aokigahara, or Sea of Trees, near Lake Sai. This forest is considered a home to ghosts, or *yūrei*, in Japanese mythology. Its living creatures include the Asian black bear, Japanese squirrel, Japanese mink, and many other mammals, birds, and insects.

Green Forests

Over half of Japan is covered in forest. Evergreen forests with **broadleaf** trees grow in warm and **temperate** regions such as Honshu, Shikoku, and Kyushu. **Coniferous** forests of fir and spruce trees are dominant in mountainous areas. **Deciduous** forests of beech and oak trees grow in cooler areas such as southern Hokkaido. Some warmer islands of the south, such as Okinawa, have mangrove forests and subtropical rain forests. Japan has a well-established forest industry, with many forests owned or managed by paper or construction companies. These forests are managed so that they can grow trees for future use.

The Japanese black bear is a sub-species of the Asian black bear. Habitat destruction and **poaching** have made their numbers decline.

Mangroves are trees that grow in coastal areas. The mangrove forests in Japan are home to unique ecosystems with diverse plants and animals.

Closer Look

Sefa-utaki is an Okinawan sacred grove that was a place of worship for the Indigenous Ryukyuan people for thousands of years. It later became a Shinto shrine and is now also a UNESCO World Heritage Site.

Japan has passed laws to prevent clear-cutting of forests to preserve trees and forest wildlife.

Sacred Groves

Sacred groves, or *Goshinboku*, are protected trees that surround shrines and temples throughout Japan. Some are large forests while others can be single trees. Sacred grove trees are usually very old and tall trees located near old village entrances and kept as homes for local guardian spirits. They are religiously important, but they also serve as forest **preserves** for animal and plant life.

1,000-year-old Goshinboku trees stand at Fujiyoshida, a city near the Fuji Five Lakes.

Coastal Living

The makeup of Japan's landscape means that most people live along the coastline in heavily populated urban centers. In addition to the capital and largest city Tokyo, mainland Japan is home to many other major cities with populations above 2 million. Many smaller cities and towns hug the coast as well. Tsunamis are one of the dangers of living close to the coastline in Japan. Tsunami is a Japanese word that means "harbor wave."

Concrete barriers, such as this one in a Japanese fishing village, can help provide protection from tsunamis.

Power of Tsunamis

Japan's **geology** means it has frequent earthquakes. Earthquakes that take place under ocean plates, or volcanoes that erupt there, can set off tsunamis. These giant waves travel inland. They grow higher closer to shore as the depth of the ocean decreases. Japan has experienced many earthquakes and tsunamis in its history. Japan's first documented earthquake took place in the year 599. Historic records show it destroyed buildings on Honshu. Large tsunamis in 1896, 1933, and 1960 killed thousands of people. They forced the country to rethink its protection plans to manage the risk of disasters. Some of those protections are physical structures. Others are warning systems and escape plans for people in the tsunami's path.

Most buildings in Japan are built with materials that allow them to absorb the shock of an earthquake. But it is difficult to build structures that can withstand powerful tsunamis.

Breakwaters, like this one on Hokkaido, are structures built around coasts to protect against waves, currents, and **storm surges**. Japan has some of the deepest breakwaters in the world.

The 2011 earthquake and tsunami also caused great destruction in the city of Fukushima.

Shakes and Waves

The Great Sendai Earthquake, or Tohuku Earthquake, in 2011 was a magnitude 9.0 earthquake centered near the city of Sendai on northern Honshu. It was the strongest in Japan's known history and set off a tsunami that produced waves up to 132 feet (40 m) high. This tsunami destroyed buildings and infrastructure such as bridges, roads, and power plants. It killed more than 18,000 people and left 450,000 homeless. It also caused a **meltdown** at the Fukushima Daiichi Nuclear Power Plant. Called the Fukushima Disaster, it released **radioactive** materials into the environment.

Scientists in protective suits measure the **radiation** levels in a danger zone around the Fukushima Daiichi Nuclear Power Plant after the meltdown.

Variable Climates

Few countries have as varied a climate as Japan. That's because the islands of Japan extend south to north through six climate zones and subzones, from subtropical to **subarctic**. The climate is also influenced by the bodies of water that surround the archipelago, and the elevations of the mountains. Japan experiences shifts in precipitation year-round. The rainy season begins in May in Okinawa in the south. It moves north through most of Honshu in June and into Hokkaido by late July. It is followed by hot, humid summers. Winter in Japan lasts from December to March. During winter, the climate ranges from pleasantly warm in the Ryukyu Islands in the south to cold and snowy in northwest Honshu and in Hokkaido.

Summers in the cities can be sticky and humid. People use umbrellas to protect themselves from the Sun. In some areas of Tokyo, mist is sprayed to cool people down.

There are hundreds of ski resorts in Japan. The country is known for its excellent winter snow conditions.

Climate change is impacting Japan's plants and animals. Weather events such as **typhoons** are becoming stronger, leading to more flooding. Coral in the sea surrounding Okinawa is being bleached due to warmer water temperatures.

Climate and Biodiversity

Japan's location and climate have influenced its diverse plant and animal life. It is known as a biodiversity hotspot, with 90,000 known species and thousands more unclassified species. Japan adopted a national biodiversity strategy in the mid-2000s. It focuses on the relationship between humans and nature. The strategy laid out targets and goals for conserving land and preserving species. The goals include preserving traditional agricultural ecosystems and setting up modern wildlife management systems to protect native Japanese deer, Asian black bears, monkeys, wild boars, and birds such as great cormorants.

Ukai is a traditional Japanese fishing method that uses trained cormorants to catch river fish. A large fire on the boat lights the way.

CHAPTER 2

Becoming Japan

Amaterasu is depicted in this artwork made in the 1800s. Many myths were written about her.

Ancient to Modern

Many cultures have creation myths that tell the story of how the world began. In Japan's creation myth, two spirits or gods, called *kami*, are born from the muddy sea that covered Earth. They are Izanagi and Izanami. When these kami married, the islands of Japan and all the other kamis of nature and the sea were formed. Izanagi and Izanami had many children, but their first was a girl named Amaterasu. She was so beautiful that they decided to put her up in the sky as the Sun. Amaterasu eventually had a son who grew up to become the emperor of Japan.

Japan's creation myth is written in the *Nihon Shoki*, or Chronicles of Japan, and the *Kojiki*, or Records of Ancient Matters. These are the oldest recognized books of myths, legends, and history of Japan. They were completed in the early 700s C.E. and set out the country's official mythology. The books would influence how the country's emperors became so important through history. Japanese people no longer believe the myths to be true, but the stories of the kamis and Japan's early leaders still impact modern Japanese culture today.

Adzuki beans are still an important crop in modern Japan. Rice cultivation was introduced to Japan at the end of the Jomon period. Today, rice and adzuki beans are often served together at important meals and holidays.

Early Japan

The islands of Japan have been home to groups of humans since 30,000 B.C.E., when there was a land connection between what is now Korea. Archaeologists are still unearthing their stone tools. The first dated culture in Japan's history is the Jomon culture (10,500 to 300 B.C.E.). These people were hunter-gatherers and early farmers. They were among the first to **cultivate** the adzuki, or red mung bean. They created decorative pottery with a hard, shiny coating that is considered complex for the time period.

This stone statue is from the Jomon period.

A reconstruction of Jomon period houses can be found on Honshu.

Founding of Japan

Japan's first emperor, Jimmu, came to power in the Jomon period around 660 B.C.E. His **ascendance** is still marked today on February 11 as National Foundation Day. He is written about in the *Nihon Shoki* and the *Kojiki*, Japan's ancient books. They say Jimmu was a descendant of Amaterasu. He was said to have lived until 126 years old. Modern historians say there is little to no historical evidence that Emperor Jimmu existed at all. However, the legends and myths surrounding him may reflect some actual events in Japanese history.

A Japanese print made in the 1890s shows Emperor Jimmu with his wooden bow.

The Kashihara Shrine, in the city of Kashihara, was built in 1890 on the site the ancient books say Emperor Jimmu ascended the throne. Shrines are public places where kami are worshipped.

Japan's ancient belief system is reflected in the country's Shinto religion. In modern-day Japan, around 100,000 public shrines can be found.

Close to 85 million people in Japan identify as Buddhist. They may worship at one of the many thousands of Buddhist temples around the country.

This Shinto priest visits a shrine in the mountains.

Closer Look

Shinto and Buddhism

Japan's foundational myths blend with one of its major religions: Shinto. It is native to Japan. It developed over time, with some scholars saying from 300 B.C.E. to 300 C.E. Buddhism, Japan's other ancient religion, adapted to Shinto's emphasis on nature and balance after arriving in Japan. Buddhism was adopted from India, through China and Korea, in the 6th century C.E.

Shinto has many spirits, gods, and goddesses. Nature is important—with everything from trees to rocks, rivers, and humans having a kami. Kami can mean spirit or god. People who follow or practice Shinto may observe certain customs or traditions, but there is no firm authority that controls their beliefs and how they express them. Some follow rituals and offer prayers to kami. They may also believe some humans can become kami. Buddhism adapted to complement many Shinto traditions while emphasising the idea of the **afterlife**.

Early Japan

The Jomon period was followed by 15 other distinct periods in Japanese history from 300 B.C.E. to the present time. Some, such as the Yayoi period that followed the Jomon, encompassed thousands of years, while others were centuries or decades long. Over time, Japan grew from an agricultural civilization, with tribes and kingdoms, to an **imperial dynasty** with one family of rulers who had great power and wealth. That dynasty survives today, although in a ceremonial, non-ruling role.

Queen Himiko of Wa, the first named female ruler in Japanese history, came to power near the end of the Yayoi period.

Buddhism was introduced and spread during and after the Asuka period. The Great Buddha of Kamakura is a large bronze statue built in 1252.

Yayoi to Clan Rule

The Yayoi people were an ancient group that lived in Japan between 300 B.C.E. and 250 C.E. They were hunter-gatherers at first, and then farmers who cultivated the important rice crop using irrigation techniques they developed. Class and clan systems developed during this period, where extended families were ruled by common ancestors.

Over time, some clans became more powerful and rulers formed small, often warring kingdoms. During the Kofun period that followed the Yayoi, Japan slowly unified under the rulers of one clan—the Yamato. The Yamato state, as it was called, became very powerful during the Asuka period (538 to 710 C.E.). Different clans intermarried to strengthen the rule of the imperial house, or House of Yamato. This is the royal family of Japan. It is the oldest continuous inherited **monarchy** in the world. Historians believe, however, that many of the first emperors and empresses, beginning with Jimmu, were mythical.

This traditional samurai helmet sits on display at a museum in Matsue, Japan.

Closer Look

Samurai Warriors

The samurai, or *bushi*, were a warrior class who were paid by the daimyo. Over time, they gained great power themselves. They were known for their battle and sword skills, and martial arts fighting tactics. Samurai warriors stopped invasions by the great Mongol warrior-ruler of China, Kublai Khan, in 1274 and 1281. Samurai were also known for their loyalty to their daimyo and clan and their code of honor, called *bushidō*.

The samurai held positions of power and respect for hundreds of years, until they were abolished in the 1870s.

A *busho* was a Japanese military commander. Bushos were active in the Sengoku or "Warring States" period (1467–1573 C.E.).

Clans and Politics

For several centuries, the power of the imperial house decreased while clans fought over rule. By the late 1100s, wars between clans brought about a period of control through military clan rulers called shoguns. They were army commanders approved by House of Yamato emperors. The shogun controlled the *daimyo*. They were a group of powerful landowners and warlords who ruled over groups of peasants.

The shogunate, or government of the shogun, held power through several periods of Japanese history from about 1185 until 1868. This was a time of clan battles and wars to gain power. Outside forces also tried to influence or gain power over Japan. The Mongols attempted to invade twice in the 1200s, and European empires sent trade expeditions.

American naval officer Matthew Perry made two gunboat expeditions to Japan in 1853 and 1854 to force Japan to sign trade agreements.

The Last Shogun

In 1867, the 15th and final shogun, Tokugawa Yoshinobu, failed to reform the failing shogunate system. This led to a **civil war** between the shogunate and forces loyal to the emperor. Known as the Boshin War, it ended the shogunate.

For 220 years, the shogunate had cut Japan off from the outside world. But in 1854, it was forced by American **gunboats** to open for trade. Japan was made to sign unequal treaties with western nations, stripping it of control over its foreign trade and criminal courts. With the collapse of the shogun system, the imperial family was restored to power.

The Meiji period (1868–1912) that followed saw the introduction of modern infrastructure, such as railway lines, and **industrialization**. The Meiji period was also a time of war, with invasions and **occupations** of Korea and war with China and Russia.

Japan was the largest **exporter** of silk in the world from the 1890s to the 1930s.

The atomic bomb was a nuclear weapon that had never before been used on humans. It proved devastating.

Taisho and Showa Periods

Japan's industrialization continued into the Taisho period (1912–1926) and the Showa period (1926–1989). However, in 1923, one of the worst earthquakes in the world destroyed Tokyo and killed 140,000 people. It was followed by a worldwide **depression** in 1929. Japan struggled through these events. Its government was then controlled by the military. In 1931, it invaded and occupied Manchuria, a region of China. By 1937, it launched another war against China. In 1940, during World War II, Japan sided with Germany and Italy. It launched a surprise attack on the United States at Pearl Harbor, Hawaii, which brought the U.S. into the war in 1941.

War and Destruction

For four years, Japan waged long and bloody war against the U.S. and the **allies** on all fronts in the Pacific. To end the war decisively, the U.S. dropped atomic bombs on the Japanese cities of Hiroshima and Nagasaki on August 6 and 9, 1945. The bombs killed 70,000 people in Hiroshima and 40,000 in Nagasaki, and injured thousands of others. This action forced Japan to surrender on August 14, 1945. The end of the war brought major changes that shaped a new Japan.

Emperor Hirohito, known in Japan as the Showa emperor, ruled from 1926 to 1989.

CHAPTER 3 Life Today

Emperor Hirohito (right) is pictured with U.S. General MacArthur after WWII. He continued to serve as emperor until 1989, but only as a "symbol" of Japan, with no ruling power.

Japan was in ruins after World War II. Its major cities were destroyed. Three million Japanese people had died and many were starving. Emperor Hirohito, a human once believed to be a descendant of the sun goddess, was forced to surrender. A seven-year-long (1945–1952) occupation began at the end of the war. Led by the American military, hundreds of thousands of allied troops oversaw massive changes in Japan.

The occupation was difficult and painful for the Japanese people. It also transformed the country. The Japanese military was disbanded—with armed forces reestablished in 1954. Shinto was abolished as the state religion. A new **constitution** was passed. Women gained the right to vote, the education system was changed, and conditions for workers were improved by new labor laws. Land reforms also took a portion of agricultural land out of the hands of the wealthy. This allowed farmers who had worked the land of rich landowners to now buy it themselves.

Customers in Tokyo after WWII line up at a food stall with signs that say it has no rice. Food shortages were common after WWII.

Major Japanese exports include machine parts, electronics, and precious metals.

Japan is the world's third-largest automobile manufacturer.

Much of Toyko was destroyed by bombing during WWII.

Economic Miracle

The transformation that brought Japan from war-torn to economic powerhouse has been called the Japanese Economic Miracle. It made Japan a world leader in **innovation**. Before the war, Japan was a mostly farm-based economy, with a growing industrial sector. After, it quickly became one of the wealthiest nations in the world. Massive growth encouraged industries that emphasized technology such as automobile, computer, and robotics manufacturing. All of this happened in less than 50 years. The new wealth brought changes in Japan's culture and in how people lived. Apartment blocks in big cities replaced village homes. People had more money to live and spend on entertainment and leisure.

Japan is a democracy, led by a prime minister. However, one party has been dominant in government since the 1950s.

Women make up less than 10 percent of lawmakers in the Japanese parliament's lower house. That number is slowly increasing.

Lost Decades

From 1978 to 2010, Japan was the world's second-largest economy. But the record growth didn't last. In the early 1990s, a **recession** began. What followed was called "the lost decades." This was a time of low economic growth, made worse by expensive natural disasters such as a massive earthquake and tsunami in 2011. It has been a long and slow economic recovery for the country, which dipped to become the third-largest economy.

The 2011 earthquake was the most powerful ever recorded in Japan.

Shinkansen "bullet trains" look like jets on train tracks. This network of high-speed electric trains connects different regions of Japan with Tokyo. As people move out of crowded cities, the number of people who commute to work on shinkansen is rising.

In 2018, Toyota launched its **hydrogen**-fueled electric Sora buses in Tokyo.

Japanese-designed vehicles are known for their reliability and efficiency.

Work in Japan

Japan's aging workforce was forced to slowly adjust to new realities. In the post-war Economic Miracle, men were the majority of the workforce. They worked long hours away from home in jobs that gave them lifetime security. Most workers commute to jobs in cities. The country has the longest working hours in the world. This means a lot of worker stress—so much so that there is even a word for workers who die from work-related stress or heart attacks: *karoshi* or "death by overwork."

Population decline is changing the way people work. It may soon require bringing more foreign workers, women, and older workers into the labor force. Women in Japan have equal rights under law, but traditional **gender roles** are still common. For example, women are less likely to continue working full time after having children.

Future Innovation

Japan is home to some of the most well-known manufacturing and technology companies in the world. They have brought about innovations such as mass-produced laptop computers, camera and robotic equipment, and more. Major technology companies, such as Sony and Nintendo, produce electronics and games. Sony is also one of the world's largest music producers and film studios. The Japanese automotive industry is one of the largest in the world. Japanese-designed vehicles have won World Car of the Year awards many times.

Kobe beef from Wagyu cattle is a specialty product known around the world. Wagyu cattle are raised in a specific region of Honshu.

Japan has one of the largest fishing industries in the world, at $14 billion per year.

Farming the Land

Farming, fishing, forestry, and mining are small but important parts of Japan's economy. Farming is one area where women outnumber men—and they are leading three-quarters of new farm business. Most are small family farms, but Japan also has farm organizations. Some use "smart agriculture" technology systems with robotic sorting machines. Rice is the most important crop, along with soybeans, sugar beets, and vegetables. Japan's mountainous geography means there is only 19,000 square miles (49,000 sq. km) of land that can be farmed. That's just 13.2 percent of the country's total land area.

Fishing and Whaling

As an island nation, Japan has more than 2,000 fishing ports. Coastal fishing, deep-sea fishing, and fish farming contribute to Japan's economy and culture. The average person in Japan eats 154 pounds (69.8 kg) of fish and seafood per year. Japan is also a whaling country. Some fishing communities have hunted whales on a small scale for hundreds of years. Today, Japan's fishing fleet includes factory ships, or fish-processing ships. On these ships, fishers can gut and freeze fish or whales on a massive scale while at sea thousands of miles away. Japan's *Nisshin Maru* is the world's only remaining whaling factory ship.

Rice is a culturally important staple food in Japan. It has been cultivated for thousands of years on terraces such as these.

Daisugi is a word that means "platform cedar." The technique is hundreds of years old.

Closer Look

Ancient Sustainable Forestry

Forestry is a small but culturally important industry in Japan. Two-thirds of Japan's land is forest, making it one of the most forested countries in the world in terms of forest to land ratio. About 40 percent of that is planted trees used for lumber. *Daisugi* is an ancient Japanese forestry technique that involves pruning the branches of a type of cedar tree so that the shoots grow straight upward and can be harvested every 20 years. This saves the rest of the tree base and roots.

The *Nisshin Maru* sits at a port in Kagoshima, Japan. Environmentalists have criticized Japan's whaling as **unsustainable**, particularly in Antarctic territory.

CHAPTER 4 A Vibrant Culture

The Ainu people traditionally lived on Hokkaido and northeast Honshu. Few speak their native language today.

This traditional Japanese wedding takes place at a Shinto shrine in Tokyo. The groom wears a five-layer kimono, the national dress of Japan. A *shiromuku*, or all-white kimono, is the dress of the bride.

Ethnicities of Japan

Japanese culture is one of the most influential cultures in the world. Japanese food, art, mythology, sports, movies, music, and fashion have influenced the world and how it views Japan today.

At various times in its history, Japan has been an isolated country geographically and culturally. This heightened outside interest in Japan. Approximately 97 percent of Japan's population is ethnically Wajin. These are the descendants of the earliest people, who arrived from East and Southeast Asia, and the Jomon people. The rest of the population is made up of smaller Indigenous groups—including the Ainu, Ōbeikei Islanders, Nivkh or Gilyak, and Ryukyuans of Okinawa—as well as ethnic Chinese, Korean, and Micronesian people.

Choosing Citizenship

Citizenship in Japan is tied to blood or Japanese ethnicity instead of birth. Japan has a small number of foreign residents who make up about 2.3 percent of the population. These are people who have come from other countries to work, often long term, in Japan. Non-Japanese people can become citizens if they have lived in Japan for a long time, but they must give up their first nationality or dual citizenship. Children who were born in Japan, but with a second citizenship, must choose Japanese citizenship by age 20.

A *torii* is a Japanese gate found at a Shinto shrine. It represents the crossing into a sacred space. The Itsukushima Shrine is known for its torii gate, which seems to float over the water.

Religion and Beliefs

Today, Japan's most followed religions are Shinto and Buddhism. They have even merged in many ways. This is known as *Shinbutsu-shugo*. For example, many Japanese people worship both at Shinto shrines and Buddhist temples, which can be built together. Other Japanese people follow the Christian religion, which was introduced to Japan by Europeans in the 1500s. There are also small groups of people who follow other world religions such as Islam, Bahá'í, Judaism, and Hinduism. The Ryukyuan and Ainu people also have their own belief systems.

Kinkaku-ji, a Buddhist temple in Kyoto, is known as the "Golden Pavilion" for its beautiful gold-covered exterior.

A kimono is made with long pieces of fabric—usually silk for formal wear.

Housing

Due to the population density of some major cities like Tokyo, housing can be found in the form of *manshon*, *apaato*, and even micro-housing. An apaato is typically a two-story building, with about 10 apartments inside. A manshon is larger, with three or more stories, and has more space. Micro-housing has a very small and compact living space—about the size of three tatami mats. These mats are about 3 by 6 feet (0.9 by 1.8 m). They are a common way to measure space in Japan.

Traditional and Modern

The traditional and modern exist close together in Japan. Women dressed in kimonos might be walking down a busy city street with men and women in expensive business suits and teenagers in hoodies or cosplay outfits. None of the clothing is out of place—it's just how people in Japan live, with lines blurred between the past, present, and future.

Kimonos date back to about 300 C.E., when the Japanese royal court adopted the garment from visiting representatives of the Chinese royal court. People still wear them today, most often for formal occasions such as weddings. Other traditional Japanese clothing includes padded winter coats known as *hanten*, short silk or cotton jackets called *haori*, or men's robes known as *nagajuban*. The common element in traditional Japanese clothing is melding the complex with simple, or minimalist design. That has carried through to some modern Japanese fashion designers such as Yohji Yamamoto, Rei Kawakubo, and Hanae Mori. Mori's designs featured flowy kimonos.

An apaato residence

Many traditional Japanese homes are built with simple lines. They are wooden structures with sliding doors and **partitions** instead of walls. Tatami mats are laid on the floor.

The Nakagin Capsule Tower in Ginza, Tokyo, is an example of a style of architecture used for living spaces today.

There were once thousands of geisha, but today they number about 1,000 and work in the larger cities such as Tokyo and Kyoto.

Geisha train for years in an apprenticeship system.

Closer Look

Geisha Culture

Geisha have a long history in Japan, dating back more than two centuries. They are female professional entertainers or "women of art." Geisha sang, played instruments, danced, and talked with male guests at tea or banquet houses in districts called *hanamachi*. Together, all hanamachi belong to the *karyūkai*, meaning "the flower and willow world." Over time, they became fashion and style icons. Their traditional white foundation makeup, red lips, and colorful silk kimonos were recognizable as a symbol of Japan. Today, geisha are known as successful businesswomen who run the karyūkai.

CHAPTER 4

Celebrations Around Japan

Many celebrations take place at Japan's Shinto shrines and Buddhist temples. Local festivals and celebrations are a large part of Japanese culture. Also known as *matsuri*, these annual community events mark the changing seasons or historical or religious events. Matsuri celebrations can include floats and elaborate parades, contests, and often special foods.

Setsubun is an annual festival held every February. It refers to the day just before the first day of spring in the traditional Japanese calendar. One focus of Setsubun is cleansing rituals. These are meant to push away bad luck and any evil spirits from the previous year.

Other festivals celebrate significant days in Japanese history, such as National Foundation Day on February 11, which commemorates the beginning of Japan's democracy after WWII in 1947. *Midori no Hi*, or Greenery Day, celebrates the nature of Japan.

Cherry blossom festivals are some of the most widely attended in Japan. They are held throughout the country at blossom time, anywhere from January to May.

Dancers perform during *Kagurazaka Matsuri*, a summer festival held in Tokyo.

Winter or snow festivals are popular in the northern regions of Japan. These festivals, including the famous Sapporo Snow Festival, feature Japanese snow huts, or *kamakura*.

Regional Foods

What goes with festivals? Food, of course. Food stalls known as *yatai* line parks and paths during festivals. They sell easy-to-eat dishes such as yakisoba noodles, pancake battered treats such as *okonomiyaki*, or even fried chicken or squid. Shave ice, or *kakigori*, is a favorite at summer festivals. This treat dates back more than 1,000 years. It helps beat the steamy weather of Japan's summers. But Japanese cuisine isn't just for festivals—the country is known the world over for its traditional foods developed in different regions and perfected over centuries.

Mochi stuffed with a sweet filling is called *daifuku*. It is often served with green tea, another Japanese staple.

Japan grows 8.21 million tons (7.45 million metric tons) of rice per year. Many Japanese foods are accompanied by rice or made from different types of rice. These include sushi, rice vinegar, and sweets such as mochi—a sweet ball made from steamed and pounded rice. The making of saké, a Japanese rice wine, likely dates back to 500 B.C.E.

Ramen is a popular noodle dish served in a broth with different meats and vegetables. Regional variations are made throughout Japan.

Traditional sushi is any dish made with Japanese rice seasoned with rice vinegar. It is often accompanied by a range of ingredients, especially raw seafood.

Arts and Crafts

Traditional Japanese arts and crafts are known for their clean lines, delicate and dramatic color, and expert **precision**. Pottery and porcelain are some of the oldest Japanese art forms. Some works have survived from the Jomon period. Ceramics are part of the *chadō*, or Japanese tea ceremony, where powdered green tea called matcha is prepared and presented to guests. The ceremony evolved over several centuries as a Buddhist practice. Many of Japan's arts and crafts, such as bonsai—the art of growing and sculpting miniature trees in containers—have ancient roots. Others, such as anime and manga, are modern interpretations of animation and cartoon drawing.

This Japanese master potter works at his wheel.

Eye for Anime

Anime is a 20th century artform that was developed in Japan when filmmakers experimented with animation styles from Europe and North America. Originally hand-drawn and now often computer-created, anime is distinctively Japanese. Over time, many different anime design styles developed with different names. Anime is used in manga, the Japanese comic books and graphic novels that developed in Japan in the 1950s. The anime industry includes more than 430 production companies and studios in Japan, many of which produce films and cartoons.

Special tools and skills are needed to craft miniature bonsai trees and plants.

Manga also has its roots in illustrated Japanese scrolls of the 1600s.

Shodo means "way of writing."

Closer Look

Schoolchildren compete in a calligraphy contest during a festival in 2016.

Shodo Calligraphy

Japanese calligraphy, or *shodo*, was introduced through China in the 500s C.E. and evolved over time. It is commonly practiced by **Zen** Buddhist monks, who believe that there is a strong connection between writing and the mind and soul. Since the brush strokes can't be corrected, the calligrapher has to have a clear mind for the lines to flow out onto the paper. Japanese calligraphy brushes are traditionally made from bamboo and animal hair.

A contemporary Godzilla monster head appears above a movie theater in Tokyo.

Popular Culture

Godzilla, Pikachu, Pokémon, Sailor Moon, karaoke, sumo...many aspects of Japanese **popular culture** are big and vibrant. Godzilla might be Japan's most famous modern monster. Although not a real monster, Godzilla is a **metaphor** for the destruction done by the nuclear weapons dropped during WWII on the cities of Hiroshima and Nagasaki. First created for a 1954 film, Godzilla and other monsters that followed became major movie characters embraced by the entire world.

Japan is also known for its "pocket monsters" called Pokémon. The manga characters were originally created for video games in 1996. Ancient Japanese mythology is filled with monster characters called *yōkai*. Many are part of village **folklore**. Some have also been painted by artists, borrowed as characters in fiction books, and featured in Japanese theater.

Monster Size

Sumo wrestling is Japan's national sport. Its history dates back thousands of years. Some ancient drawings depicted sumo as a ritual dance prayer for a good harvest season. Today, sumo wrestling matches are major events that take place in stadiums on a *dohyō*, or an elevated ring covered in sand. Rituals are also a part of sumo matches. For example, at the beginning of a match, wrestlers stomp and slap their knees and stomachs to scare evil spirits away.

Japanese martial arts include kendo (right), judo, jujitsu, and many others.

Sumo wrestlers, also known as *rikishi*, line up at a tournament in Tokyo. Wrestlers cannot exit the dohyo or touch the ground with any body part other than the soles of the feet. The first one to do this loses the match.

Making costumes and impersonating characters is a hobby for many youths in Japan.

Character Dressing

Cosplay, or dressing up as a favorite character from manga, anime, and video games, is not unusual for youths and teens in some Japanese cities. Japanese dress-up culture allows young people to take on different identities for fun. Style varies from city to city and even district to district and year to year. It's about fitting in with a crowd.

Karaoke Kan is a large karaoke chain in Japan. Karaoke is a form of live entertainment where people sing along to popular songs with a microphone and taped music. It had its beginnings in Japan in the 1960s and 1970s.

CHAPTER 5 Looking to the Future

Government incentives in Japan encourage city-dwelling families to move to small towns and villages. The idea is to have younger people repopulate areas with declining populations, and also support the elderly living in these areas.

Japan's future, like its history and culture, is tied to its geography. Its physical geography, including the sea, mountains, volcanoes, and greenery, has influenced how people live and view the world around them. Culturally, many Japanese values are rooted in the land and the concept of *ma*. Ma means pause, space, or gap. It plays out in different aspects of Japanese life, such as the design of traditional buildings and gardens. It also informs beliefs and actions, such as the way many Japanese people bow and pause respectfully upon meeting and greeting others.

Population Decline

While the world's population is increasing, Japan's is decreasing. This has alarmed politicians who believe that if things don't change, Japan will not be able to maintain a functioning society. A growing population is necessary to work and pay the taxes needed for government services such as transportation, schools, and care homes for the elderly. One solution is to encourage immigration from other countries—something less common in Japan than other countries.

Japanese seniors read newspapers while commuting on a train. Japan has the longest life expectancy in the world, and a declining youth population.

Japan is helping answer the problem of its shrinking workforce by adding more automated jobs.

Japan's cities are investing in design features that make public transportation accessible, such as adding wheelchair lifts and ramps to train stations.

Tradition and Change

Rapid economic change and growth post-WWII brought Japan from disaster to the world's second-largest developed country in four decades. The slow growth that followed the Economic Miracle was a period of economic difficulty, but also a time when many Japanese people reported life satisfaction. Part of this may be due to how Japan's government increased social supports.

Now, with the highest proportion of elderly people in the world, Japan is aiming to stabilize its workforce for the future and make cities and villages easier to live in. This includes "age-friendly" housing, traffic and disaster safety, and better public transport for people with disabilities. One way Japanese cities are becoming more age-friendly is by recycling unused buildings, such as closed schools, into care facilities. Another example is making sure public walkways are accessible.

Megacity Future

Despite its declining and rapidly aging population, Japan is still one of the most densely populated countries in the world. Tokyo is on track to having the world's highest population density by 2030. As a center of manufacturing, with many skyscrapers, Tokyo uses a lot of energy and creates a lot of waste. In summer, Tokyo becomes a "heat island" where the air temperature is higher than the suburbs. The city is combating this with solar heat-blocking pavement, planting more trees along roadways, and water sprinkler systems to cool the city and pavement. Future projects include floating solar farms in Tokyo Bay to provide renewable energy.

Pollution Pressures

Megacities and high population density puts pressure on the country's waste-management systems. Japan generates a lot of waste, including plastic waste. Landfill space is limited, and two-thirds of the country's trash is burned. Japan is researching ways to both avoid waste and deal better with it. Some of these include nature-based solutions that combat climate change.

The town of Kamikatsu on the island of Shikoku is an example. It has become a zero-waste leader by sending 80 percent of its trash through a **circular economy** system that involves the entire town. People help recycle, give to a thrift shop, and remake or upcycle donated items. Even the local brewery makes beer from farm leftovers, or crops that are misshapen. Leftover grain is made into farm fertilizer. A volunteer rideshare system limits the number of cars in the town as residents share vehicles. Other towns and cities in Japan are learning from Kamikatsu's success and planning similar systems.

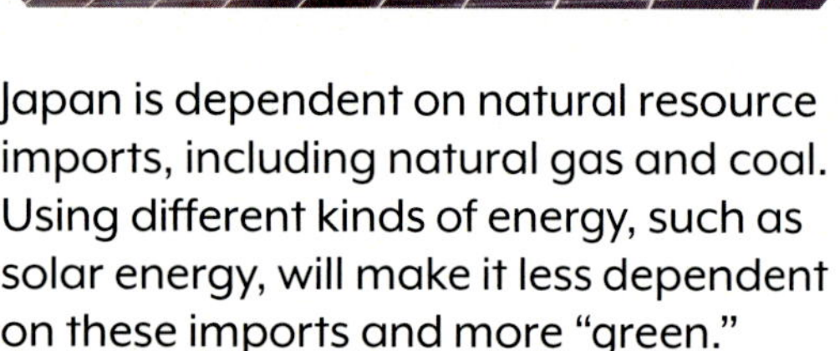

Japan is dependent on natural resource imports, including natural gas and coal. Using different kinds of energy, such as solar energy, will make it less dependent on these imports and more "green."

Tokyo's urban sprawl, or rapid outward expansion, has been an issue for decades.

Combating Climate Change

Japan's island ecosystems face challenges from global warming and rising sea levels, as well as disappearing coral reefs. Rising sea levels and stronger typhoons due to climate change threaten cities such as Osaka, which has $200 billion worth of real estate near sea level and canals that run through its tourist area. Osaka's Global Warming Action Plan includes reducing **greenhouse gas** emissions and strengthening infrastructure to resist sea-level rise.

High temperatures due to climate change are making it more difficult to grow rice in Japan.

New Japan

Toyota Woven City in Susono, Japan, is a test city to show how a future "smart city" might work. It is being built with robots, artificial intelligence, self-driving cars, pedestrian and cyclist roads, hydrogen power, and other innovative technology. The aim is to use solar and geothermal energy for all energy and power sources. It also aims to create an infrastructure that allows people to move around the city easily.

Upcycling involves taking discarded objects and materials and remaking them into useful new items.

Japan's government has pledged to promote and finance green innovation as a key way to combat climate change.

accessible Able to be reached

afterlife Life after death

allies In WWII, the 26 nations, including Britain, Canada, and the U.S., that fought against the Axis powers, including Germany and Japan

ascendance The act of rising up or taking a position or throne

broadleaf A plant with wide, flat leaves

circular economy A way of consuming that involves sharing, repairing, recycling, and reusing things

civil war A war between two groups within the same country

climate change A long-term change in the temperatures and weather patterns on Earth. Climate change often refers to global warming.

commercial Relating to buying and selling goods

commute To travel between one's home and place of work

coniferous Evergreen trees

constitution A country's basic principles and laws

cultivate To prepare land and grow and harvest crops

deciduous Trees that shed their leaves annually

depopulating Reducing or removing the population

depression A period of long-term economic downturn, usually lasting years

efficient Able to complete a task without extra time, effort, or resources

exporter A country, person, or company that sends goods to another country

folklore The traditions, beliefs, and stories shared by a community

gender roles How males and females are stereotypically expected to act in a society

geology The science that studies the physical history of Earth and its processes

geothermal Energy that comes from heat within Earth

gradients Inclined surfaces

greenhouse gas A gas, such as carbon dioxide, that traps heat in Earth's atmosphere

gunboats Small, armed warships used in ports where the water is shallow

hydrogen A colorless and odorless gas

imperial dynasty The ruling of a country or region by one family for generations

Indigenous People who are the original or earliest known inhabitants of a region and their descendants

industrialization The process by which a society changes from mostly agricultural to more industrial

industry Economic activity related to collecting and processing raw materials

innovation Creating something new or different

irrigation Systems used to supply water for crops

meltdown The accidental melting of a nuclear reactor core due to overheating

metaphor Something used to represent something else, such as a symbol

metropolis A very large city

monarchy A government led by a monarch, such as a king, queen, or emperor

native Natural to a place

occupation The military control of one country or territory by another

paddies Partially flooded fields where rice is grown

partitions Structures that divide a space

plains Large areas of flat land with few or no trees

poaching Illegally hunting or catching animals

popular culture Cultural artifacts that reflect the tastes of the general public in a given culture at a given time

populous Heavily populated

precision Being careful, exact, and accurate

preserves Places that protect animals or plants

radiation Energy that comes from a nuclear reaction and is dangerous to health

radioactive Emitting radiation

recession A significant drop in economic activity lasting months

sacred Connected to gods or religion

shrine In Japan, a public place where kami are worshipped

Soviet Union Name for the Union of Soviet Socialist Republics, a group of countries across Eurasia formed in 1922 and dissolved in 1991

storm surges Abnormal rise in sea level during a storm

subarctic Region immediately south of the Arctic Circle, with long, cold winters

subtropical Regions that border tropical areas, or areas around the equator, with hot, humid summers

tectonic plates Huge masses of rock that form Earth's crust

temperate Having mild temperatures

typhoon A tropical cyclone that develops in the northern hemisphere

UNESCO World Heritage Site A protected landmark or area singled out by the United Nations Educational, Scientific, and Cultural Organization as being globally significant

uninhabited Not lived in by people

unsustainable Unable to be continued at the same rate

World War II The 1939–1945 war between the Axis powers (Germany, Japan, and Italy) and the Allies (mainly the UK and its colonies, the U.S., and the Soviet Union)

Zen A form of Buddhism in Japan that focuses on meditation

Books

Ancient Japan for Kids. Captivating History, 2021.

Arato, Rona. *Fukushima Nuclear Disaster*. Crabtree Publishing, 2014.

Norbury, Paul. *Japan—Culture Smart! The Essential Guide to Customs & Culture*. Kuperard, 2021.

Websites

https://www.japan-guide.com
Take a look at the regions of Japan, its weather, a map, and interesting stories about Japanese cities, markets, and culture.

https://kids.nationalgeographic.com/geography/countries/article/japan
Discover simple, at-a-glance information about the country, including the people, nature, and forms of government.

http://afe.easia.columbia.edu/timelines/japan_timeline.htm
Check out this easy-to-follow timeline of Japan's historical periods and dynasties.

https://web-japan.org/
Visit the Web Japan site for all kinds of information about Japan's geography and culture. Explore videos, activities, maps, and articles about topics from vending machines to fashion trends, anime, and oyster farming.

About the Authors

Ellen Rodger is an author of over 50 books for children and young people. She has an intimate knowledge of Japanese snack foods, acquired from years spent hunched at her desk snacking while writing

Anne-Marie Rodger is an author of several books for children and a fan of Taylor Swift music. She enjoys spending time with her husband and their standard poodle, Jagger.